TOMATO

LIFE CYCLES

T0106014

Words that look like **this** can be found in the glossary on page 24.

BookLife
PUBLISHING

©2021
BookLife Publishing Ltd.
King's Lynn
Norfolk PE30 4LS

All rights reserved.
Printed in Malaysia.

A catalogue record for this book is available from the British Library.

ISBN: 978-1-83927-161-8

Written by:
Kirsty Holmes

Edited by:
Shalini Vallepur

Designed by:
Danielle Webster-Jones

CONTENTS

LIFE CYCLES

WHAT IS A LIFE CYCLE?

All animals, plants and humans go through different stages of their life as they grow and change. This is called a life cycle.

Human life cycle

 Baby  **Child** **Adult**

WHAT IS A TOMATO?

A tomato is a type of plant. The tomato plant has a thick stem and small flowers. The tomato is the soft, round fruit of the plant.

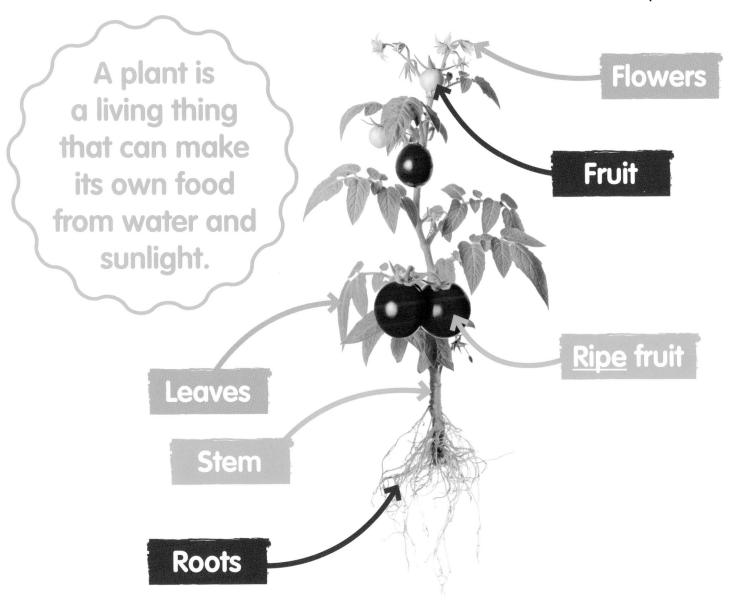

A plant is a living thing that can make its own food from water and sunlight.

Flowers

Fruit

Ripe fruit

Leaves

Stem

Roots

SEEDS

Tomato seeds are small and pale. One end is round and the other is pointy. They like to grow in warm soil. The seeds contain food that helps the plant to grow.

Tomato seeds

Seeds are found inside ripe fruits. Farmers **harvest** ripe fruits and use the seeds inside to grow new tomatoes. Tomatoes are easy to grow in containers in gardens.

Fruit

Tomato seeds need soil, water, warmth and sunlight to grow.

Seeds

SPROUTS

The seed will grow a root down into the soil. This first root is called a radicle. The radicle takes in **nutrients** from the soil. Then the seed grows a small stem and two small leaves called seed leaves.

This is called a sprout.

Tomato plants grow very quickly if the <u>conditions</u> are right.

The stem of this sprout is called a plumule. It will become the main stem of the plant. The leaves take in sunlight and make food to help the sprout grow.

LEAVES

The true leaves of the tomato plant are large and dark green with jagged edges. As these leaves grow, the tomato plant's stem will grow into a long, thick vine.

True leaf

Vine

There are two types of tomato plant. Determinate plants grow to their full size of around one and a half metres and then stop. Indeterminate plants will grow and grow… and grow!

FLOWERS

Tomato flowers are small and yellow. Tomato flowers have both male and female parts.

Petals

Pollen

Bees and other insects take the pollen from the male parts of the flower to the female parts. This is called pollination. Wind may also blow the pollen from the male parts to the female parts.

A tiny green ball will then grow inside the flower.

TOMATOES

The tiny green balls are tomato fruits. At first, they are green. They slowly get bigger and turn yellow, orange or red.

Tomatoes need warmth from the Sun so they can become ripe.

Seeds

Tomatoes are delicious to eat when they are ripe. The fruit will be full of new seeds, ready to be planted next year.

TYPES OF TOMATO

Not all tomatoes are red. Tomatoes come in all sorts of colours.
They can be green, yellow, orange, striped, white and even black!

How many different
colours can you see
in this picture?

Beefsteak tomato

Plum tomato

Cherry tomato

Tomatoes come in all different shapes and sizes, too.
Cherry tomatoes are small. Beefsteak tomatoes are big.
Plum tomatoes are usually oval-shaped.

TOMATO FACTS

Many people think tomatoes are a vegetable. This is because we eat them in salads and on pizzas – not somewhere you'd expect to find a fruit! But tomatoes are actually a fruit.

The tomato is a fruit because it has seeds.

If we didn't harvest it, eventually the tomato would fall off the vine and **<u>rot</u>**. The seeds would grow inside the fruit, using the flesh as food until they could find the soil to take root.

These seeds have sprouted inside the tomato.

WORLD RECORD BREAKERS

World's Heaviest Tomato

Weighing in at just under four kilograms, the tomato grown by Dan Sutherland holds the world record for world's heaviest tomato.

Tallest Tomato Plant

The tallest tomato plant in the world was grown in Lancashire in the UK. It was almost 20 metres tall!

LIFE CYCLE OF A TOMATO

1 The tomato seed grows a root and a sprout.

2 The sprout grows leaves and a thick stem.

LIFE CYCLES

4 The fruit grows and is full of new seeds.

3 The flowers are pollinated by insects and the wind.

GET EXPLORING!

Why not plant a tomato of your own and watch the different stages as it grows? Ask an adult to cut a tomato open and keep the seeds, ready to plant again…

GLOSSARY

conditions   the state of the environment, such as the temperature, rainfall and food available

harvest   to pick fully grown crops

nutrients   natural things that plants and animals need in order to grow and stay healthy

pollen   powder that is made by the flowers on a plant

ripe   when something has finished growing and is ready to eat

rot   to break down and decay

INDEX

PHOTO CREDITS

All images are courtesy of Shutterstock.com, unless otherwise specified. With thanks to Getty Images, Thinkstock Photo and iStockphoto.
Front cover & 1 – Tim UR. 2 – sergo1972. 3 – Miyuki Satake, Tetiana Rostopira, Natali Samorod. 4 – New Africa, New Africa, Djomas.
5 – Ailisa. 6 – FotoDuets. 7 – All for you friend. 8 – VladKK. 9 – kirillov alexey. 10 – NUM LPPHOTO. 11 – Catalin Petolea. 12 – Tim UR.
13 – Marykit, vallefrias. 14 – Kostiantyn Kravchenko. 15 – Mikhail Klyoshev. 16 – Robert Kneschke. 17 – Rob kemp, sasimoto. 18 – Liv friis-
larsen. 19 – matahiasek. 20 – DRogatnev, diluck, artem_mortem. 21 – yusufdemirci, illpos, MicroOne. 22 – NDenis Tabler, Iakov Filimonov,
Seda Bodur, Mila Atkovska. 23 – Iakov Filimonov.